THE HOLLAND AMERICA LINE

A 120th Anniversary Celebration in Postcards

PETER C. KOHLER

SHIP PICTORIAL PUBLICATIONS
1993

Cover: STATENDAM III postcard

First published in 1993 by Ship Pictorial Publications
The Cabinet, High Street, Coltishall, Norfolk NR12 7AA

© P. C. Kohler 1993

British Library Cataloguing in Publication Data
P. C. Kohler
   The Holland America Line: A 120th Anniversary Celebration in Postcards

ISBN 0 9516038 4 1

Ship Pictorial Series

Typesetting by Peter C. Kohler

Printed by Page Bros (Norwich) Ltd

A FOREWORD FROM HOLLAND AMERICA LINE

When a company can call upon an illustrious 120-year history, it gives us a record of accomplishment which we call our "Tradition of Excellence". This book is a fitting tribute to the dedicated men and women who helped make Holland America Line what it has become today. Our fleet continues to earn accolades for its consistent quality and service standards. We hope you'll find this book to be as entertaining as we did. And of course, we hope to see everyone who reads this book on a Holland America Line ship sometime soon.

A. K. "Kirk" Lanterman
President and Chief Executive Officer

ROTTERDAM V at New York.

INTRODUCTION

Holland America Line's current advertising theme "A tradition of excellence" takes on added significance in 1993 when the company celebrates its 120th anniversary. Of the major cruise lines, only Cunard, Hapag-Lloyd, P&O and Paquet can claim to be older, and none has remained truer to their past and traditions than the Dutch firm.

This book is not a history of the fleet, the operations or the business of Holland America, but rather a retrospective of the line's ships as illustrated by company-issued postcards. Why postcards? Firstly, they are often beautiful and evocative paintings of the vessels or historic photographs. Secondly, they were actually used aboard the ships represented and have a human dimension lacking in stock photos. The jottings by passengers—"rough trip, wasn't sick", "we sailed to Europe in this boat, here is our cabin" (denoted by an "X" in the appropriate position to the dismay of later card collectors)—provide a personal insight into what sea travel aboard past H.A.L. ships was like. Finally, it is hoped that this book will be of value to the growing number of ocean liner postcard collectors.

One hundred twenty postcards, a representative collection of the more than 140 vessels that flew the line houseflag, including most major classes or groups of ships for which postcards were issued, are reproduced. Holland America was quite diligent in printing various cards for its ships, from liners to freighters to passenger tenders. There are even postcards of a ship's menu, an engine room and a cabin bathroom!

Very soon passengers will be mailing a new generation of postcards from the latest sister ships STATENDAM V, MAASDAM V and RYNDAM III which in name and quality carry forth the Holland America "tradition of excellence" into the 21st century. "Having a great time, wish you were here" . . .

Peter C. Kohler
Washington, D.C.
March 1993

A SHORT HISTORY OF THE HOLLAND AMERICA LINE

"Finally a sprig becomes a tree", "The Spotless Fleet", "It's Good to be on a Well Run Ship"—Holland America's mottos over the years are a clue to a company of modest beginnings whose enduring success was not owed to record-breaking superliners or floating palace style, but rather to quiet, dependable quality, sound value, prudent and often innovative management, and the lasting virtues of good service, fine cuisine and solid comfort.

Originally known as Plate, Reuchlin & Co., founded on 8 February 1871, the line began trans-Atlantic sailings in October the following year between Flushing/Brouwershaven and New York with the 1,700-gross ton ROTTERDAM I and MAASDAM I, 10.5-knot vessels that took 16 days to cross the Atlantic. Financial problems resulted in a reorganisation and the formation on 9 April 1873 of the Nederlandsch Amerikaansche Stoomvaart Maatschappjj (NASM), known popularly as Holland America Line from 1896 onwards. Direct sailings from Rotterdam were soon made facilitated by the New Waterway which linked the Maas port with the Hook of Holland and the North Sea. In its early years the line offered sailings from both Amsterdam and Rotterdam.

Originally Holland America's principal trade was emigrants and the company, despite financial setbacks and a spate of mishaps in the 1880s, prospered from the epic European migration to America before the First World War. Both new and used tonnage was employed, including EDAM II (1883), the first steel-hulled ship built outside of Britain, and White Star Line's former BALTIC, REPUBLIC and ARABIC, which when built were among the most advanced liners of their day. ROTTERDAM II (1886) undertook Holland America's first cruise, 15–25 June 1895, Rotterdam to Copenhagen and in doing so, was the first liner to pass through the Kiel Canal.

Celebrating its first 25 years, during which H.A.L. ships had completed 1,300 voyages and carried 90,000 saloon and 400,000 steerage passengers, in 1898 the company ordered its first ship to exceed 10,000 grt and the first of a long line of Harland & Wolff-built ships for the firm, STATENDAM I.

The turn of the century also marked the dawn of a new era for Holland America, including altered funnel colours (green/white-green bands, the City of Rotterdam colours, on a buff funnel instead of black) and orders for three 12,000-grt liners and a new fleet of freighters. In 1902, 51 per cent of H.A.L.'s shares were acquired by Harland & Wolff, part of J. P. Morgan's International Mercantile Marine Company (I.M.M.) combine. Notable ships of the period included NIEUW AMSTERDAM I of 1906 and the long-serving ROTTERDAM IV of 1908.

A separate cargo service between Rotterdam and Baltimore commenced in 1909. STATENDAM I's cruise to the Mediterranean and Holy Land in 1910 introduced H.A.L. to this infant market and was followed by NIEUW AMSTERDAM I and ROTTERDAM IV. These first cruises were made under charter to travel agencies like Thos. Cook & Son, American Express and Frank C. Clark.

The Netherlands remained neutral during the First World War and H.A.L. reaped large profits by continuing its North Atlantic service although several of its ships were damaged by mines in the North Sea, and the new STATENDAM II was taken over by the British as a troopship and as JUSTICIA was sunk by U-boats in 1918, whilst other members of the fleet served as transports for the Allies. In 1917, the company reverted to full Dutch ownership. As compensation for its war losses, H.A.L. received 60,000 tons of shipbuilding materials with which to renew its cargo and passenger fleet.

The inter-war years saw new ships like the famous "V"s, VOLENDAM I and VEENDAM II, and the magnificent STATENDAM III added to the fleet along with a new fleet of "B" class freighters, but these were difficult times. STATENDAM's construction was postponed by financial losses, and it took nine years to complete the ship. United States immigration restrictions killed off most of the steerage trade, but by then H.A.L.'s quality had won it a good share of the increasing tourist and cruise traffic. Worse to come was the Depression and the company, wholly without government subsidy unlike some of its competitors, was in dire straits. The fleet was pruned of 12 vessels, either sold or laid up.

Gradual recovery, dynamic management and government loans resulted in the construction of the peerless NIEUW AMSTERDAM II of 1938, one of the 'thirties illustrious "Ships of State". A new concept in trans-Atlantic travel, the one-class combination cargo-passenger liner ("combi") was also introduced that year with NOORDAM II. The company acquired Red Star Line's PENNLAND and WESTERNLAND and its Antwerp-New York service in 1939 when Nazi policies forced owner Arnold Bernstein, a German Jew, to disband the line.

Germany's invasion of the neutral Netherlands in May 1940 resulted in STATENDAM III, DINTELDYK I and BOSCHDYK being burnt out in Rotterdam and the balance of the fleet either employed by the Allies as transports or seized by the Germans. WESTERNLAND acted as the temporary seat of the Dutch Government-in-Exile at Falmouth. The company headquarters was moved to Curacao, Netherlands West Indies, whilst Holland America ships, proudly flying the Dutch flag, carried on the fight in Allied service. Altogether six ships were lost to enemy action: PENNLAND, ZAANDAM, MAASDAM III, BREEDYK, BEEMERSTERDYK and BILDERDYK whilst WESTERNLAND was sold to the British Admiralty and ZUIDERDAM, under construction in Holland during the occupation was sunk by the Germans as a blockship and later scrapped. Nothing symbolised the hard-won victory more than NIEUW AMSTERDAM II's heroic arrival back at Rotterdam in 1946 after six years' trooping.

The late 'forties through the 'fifties were good years for ocean travel, and for Holland America. Post-war sailings were begun by the combi liner WESTERDAM, under construction during the war, and the refitted NOORDAM II, VEENDAM II and NIEUW AMSTERDAM II. Cruises, which the line had first offered before World War One and developed in the inter-war years, now played a significant role in operations. To renew its cargo operations, no fewer than 16 American-built "Victory" ships were acquired. On the Atlantic run, the company catered for the budget traveller with VOLENDAM I and the revolutionary RYNDAM II and MAASDAM IV which gave Tourist Class passengers run of the ship. The line also managed the Netherlands Government-owned GROOTE BEER which carried emigrants to North America, South Africa and Australia. Another successful budget operation was the Europe-Canada Line, H.A.L.-owned from 1963 onwards.

The often traumatic transition from crossing to cruising faced by other shipping lines in the Jet Age of the 'sixties was not experienced by Holland America. Indeed, its new flagship ROTTERDAM V of 1959 was innovatively designed for both trades with such success that after 30 years she remains in service, more popular than ever. As the trans-Atlantic service declined (NIEUW AMSTERDAM II making the last crossing in 1971), the cruise market boomed with the line offering everything from 90-day world cruises to short weekend jaunts. In 1967 the company introduced its novel "no tipping required" policy.

Celebrating its 100th anniversary, the company restyled itself as Holland America Cruises, retired the beloved NIEUW AMSTERDAM II, built its first purpose-built cruise ship (PRINSENDAM) and introduced VOLENDAM II and VEENDAM III, former U.S. flag liners, to cruise service. The company headquarters was moved from Rotterdam to the United States. The famous Indonesian service personnel were brought aboard during this time. New markets were developed, especially to Alaska where Westours was acquired, and to Bermuda, and sea/land packages were offered. The fuel crisis and inflation took its toll on company profits, however.

One of the few traditional lines to survive into the 1980s, Holland America Cruises happily reverted to "Line", revived its 'thirties logo and found an appreciative market for its classic-style cruising. STATENDAM IV of 1957 and the two "V"s were pensioned off and H.A.L. took delivery of the twins NIEUW AMSTERDAM III and NOORDAM III in 1983/4. Building on the great success of its Westours operations, the headquarters was moved from New York to Seattle, Washington. The decade was one of market expansion and line consolidation. Holland America acquired Windstar Sail Cruises and WINDSTAR, WINDSPIRIT and WINDSONG and Homes Lines' two-year-old HOMERIC in 1988 (renamed WESTERDAM II), only for the line itself to be acquired itself by the hugely successful Carnival Cruise Lines in January 1989.

Although ending a proud tradition of independent Dutch ownership, Carnival's acquisition of Holland America ensures its continued success and expansion as an independently operating subsidiary. ROTTERDAM V was extensively refitted and WESTERDAM II lengthened. Three new ships, the first to be named STATENDAM V due to enter service in 1992, followed by MAASDAM V and RYNDAM III, were ordered from Fincantieri of Italy. With these new vessels, Holland America will offer even more wide-ranging cruise itineraries whilst maintaining its ever-popular Caribbean and Alaskan routes. In 1993 ROTTERDAM V resumed her round the world cruises and STATENDAM V introduced European-based itineraries.

Known today for the traditional comfort and style of its ships, Holland America Line may look back proudly on a distinguished history. Among its notable innovations have been the inclusion of the first glass-enclosed promenade deck, the provision of private facilities in all cabins, the establishment of a "no-tipping required" policy and the development of new concepts in Alaskan cruising. The company can take pride in its 120 years of achievement and can look forward with confidence towards the future. Now, as in 1873, "It's Good to be on a Well Run Ship".

NOTES TO ILLUSTRATIONS

. All illustrations are taken from the author's collection except where otherwise noted.

. Roman numeral(s) following a ship's name indicate the first, second etc. vessel of that name in Holland America Line service.

. Dates following a ship's name indicate the length of time in Holland America Line service.

. Brief statistical details of each vessel illustrated are listed in the Index on pages 57–60.

. Tonnage shown on some illustrations may differ from that shown in the Index. This is due to modifications during a ship's career.

. The term "class" indicates that the vessel in question is one of several ships of broadly similar design. The term "sister ship(s)" indicates that these vessels were built to the same dimensions, specifications and power and were generally similar but not necessarily identical in appearance and layout.

ACKNOWLEDGEMENTS

This book could not have been produced without the generous cooperation of fellow ocean liner postcard collectors Charles N. Dragonette, Richard Maxwell, Christopher and Ellen Sterling, and Albert Watson III. In addition the author wishes to thank Gordon Turner for his helpful editing, publisher Alan S. Mallett, and Holland America Line's Director of Public Relations, Rich Skinner, APR. A special note of appreciation to Holland America Line President A. K. "Kirk" Lanterman for contributing the foreword.

(Dragonette collection)

SPAARNDAM I (1890-1901)

Built 1881 by Harland & Wolff, Belfast, as ARABIC of White Star Line. To H.A.L. 1890, renamed SPAARNDAM I. 90
First 52 Second and 694 Third Class passengers. 1901 scrapped at Preston. This early card, posted from Boulogne in 1894,
reads: "Arrived in safety, start for Rotterdam to-morrow then to Amsterdam". From 1883-1900 H.A.L. offered sailings
from both Dutch ports.
Sister ships: VEENDAM I and MAASDAM II

STATENDAM I (1898-1910)

(Sterling collection)

Built by Harland & Wolff, Belfast. 210 First 166 Second and 1020 Third Class passengers. The first Dutch liner to exceed 10,000 grt and the first of a new generation of ships, STATENDAM I is depicted on this card, posted from near sister RYNDAM I. 1910 introduced H.A.L. cruises. 1911 sold to Allan Line (SCOTIAN) and 1919 to Canadian Pacific. 1920 scrapped as MARGLEN.

Rotterdam. *Potsdam v. d. Amerika lijn.*

POTSDAM (1900-1915)   (Sterling collection)

Built by Blohm & Voss, Hamburg. 282 First 208 Second and 2000 Third Class passengers. A larger version of STATENDAM and nick-named "FUNNELDAM" after her smokestack had to be heightened 23 feet to improve draught for her coal furnaces. Became Swedish-American Line's first ship, STOCKHOLM, in 1915. Converted into a whale factory ship in 1922 and scuttled at Cherbourg in 1944. Scrapped 1947.
Sister ships: RYNDAM I and NOORDAM I

T.S.S. RIJNDAM. 12527 Tons Register. 22070 Tons Displacement.

RYNDAM I (1901-1929)

Built by Harland & Wolff, Belfast. 286 First 196 Second 1,800 Third Class passengers. Note: alternately spelled RIJNDAM. Twice damaged by mines in North Sea whilst in commercial service in World War One. 21 March 1917 taken over by United States as transport. October 1919 returned to owners. 1929 scrapped at Hendrik Ido Ambacht.
Sister ships: POTSDAM and NOORDAM I

S. S. Noordam der Holl-Amerika Lijn.   *Rotterdam.*

Uitg. P. F. v. d. Ende, Rotterdam.

NOORDAM I (1902-1927)   (Sterling collection)

Built by Harland & Wolff, Belfast. 286 First 292 Second 1,800 Third Class passengers. An early sepia-toned photo card. 1923-1926 chartered to Swedish American Line and renamed KUNGSHOLM. 1926 scrapped at Hendrik Ido Ambacht, Netherlands.
Sister ships: POTSDAM and RYNDAM I

Social Hall.

POTSDAM-class Social Hall
(Sterling collection)

Unidentified, but believed to be the First Class Social Hall of one of the three POTSDAM-type liners. Typical of Edwardian Era steamer decor, the social hall was the only public room generally used (for teas, concerts and dancing) by both ladies and gentlemen in an era when the Smoking Room was an all-male enclave.

T.S.S. NEW AMSTERDAM.

HOLLAND—AMERICA LINE.

IEUW AMSTERDAM I (1906-1932)

ilt by Harland & Wolff, Belfast. 417 First 391 Second 2,300 Third Class passengers. First quadruple expansion engined
A.L. liner and last fitted with emergency sails. This card, posted from New York on 14 August 1907, reads "We sail in
hour. I have a splendid cabin, room for 3, all to myself". This Fred Pansing painting features the Hudson River Day
ne's HENDRICK HUDSON and a fanciful tug with H.A.L. livery and houseflag.

7

HOLLAND-AMERICA LINE.

ROTTERDAM—NEW YORK
ROTTERDAM—HALIFAX (CANADA) } DIRECT SERVICE

T.S.S **NIEUW AMSTERDAM.** 17250 Tons Register - 31000 Tons Displacement.

NIEUW AMSTERDAM I (1906-1932)

(Maxwell collectic

One of the paintings by famous British maritime artist Charles Dixon c.1928, depicting the vessel sailing from her namesa
port, Nieuw Amsterdam, the original Dutch name for New York. Actually, until 1963, H.A.L.'s terminal was in Hoboke
New Jersey, the piers and ships figuring prominently in the 1953 film "On the Waterfront", starring Marlon Brando.

Dome in first class Dining Saloon.

NIEUW AMSTERDAM I (1906-1932)
(Sterling collection)

Not identified, but believed to be the First Class dining saloon of NIEUW AMSTERDAM I which extended upwards through three decks, topped by a painted glass skylight. Note the ornate, hand-carved wood panelling and the long tables with fixed swivel chairs.

9

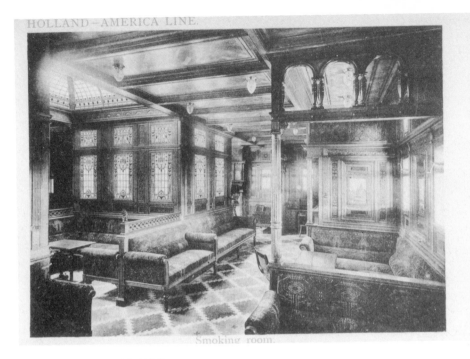

Smoking room.

NIEUW AMSTERDAM I (1906-1932)

(Sterling collection

Believed to be the First Class Smoking Room of NIEUW AMSTERDAM, a dark-panelled, stained-glass setting for the masculine pastimes of smoking, drinking and card playing. Company brochures of the time warned passengers that "professional gamblers are known to frequent trans-Atlantic steamers".

HOLLAND—AMERICA LINE.

Tender Holland leaving Boulogne s/Mer.

HOLLAND (1902-1939)

(Dragonette collection)

Built by J.T. Eltringham, South Shields. Holland America even issued postcards even for its tenders at Boulogne-sur-Mer which conveyed passengers and mail out to the liners anchored in the roadstead. The best known of these was HOLLAND which was registered under the French-flag Compagnie Franco-Hollando Americaine. 1945 sold to Chamber of Commerce, Boulogne, and out of Lloyd's Register 1962.

ROTTERDAM IV (1908-1940)
Built by Harland & Wolff, Belfast. 530 First 555 Second 2,124 Third Class passengers. The Netherland's largest ship fro
1908-1938. This is her earliest postcard and interestingly does not portray her innovative glass-enclosed promenade dec
a feature not yet envisaged when the painting was commissioned.

HOLLAND-AMERICA LINE.   ROTTERDAM - NEW YORK.

T.S.S. ROTTERDAM,   24170 Tons Register, 37190 Tons Displacement.

ROTTERDAM IV (1908-1940)

Another early card, by Fred Pansing, posted upon arrival at New York on 10 August 1909. Again the glazed promenade is not depicted. ROTTERDAM IV's First Class accommodation was superb for its day, there being 150 single staterooms and 48 cabins with private bath.

HOLLAND—AMERICA LINE. T.S.S. ROTTERDAM. 24170 Tons Register. 37190 Tons Displacement.

VESTIBULE.

ROTTERDAM IV (1908-1940)   (Dragonette collection)

First Class vestibule. ROTTERDAM IV was the first truly de luxe H.A.L. liner and famed for her ornate First Class interiors, including this magnificent staircase which introduced the ship to embarking passengers. From a set of sepia-toned interior cards sold in the ship's shop.

DINING ROOM.

ROTTERDAM IV (1908-1940)   (Dragonette collection)

First Class dining saloon with its central well, square tables and swivel chairs fastened to the deck. In the 1920s, more convivial round tables and free-standing armchairs were installed. Note the lovely shaded table lamps. In those days, dinner dress (white tie for gentlemen) was *de rigeur*, most evenings.

15

HOLLAND—AMERICA LINE. T.S.S. ROTTERDAM, 24170 Tons Register, 37190 Tons Displacement.

PROMENADE DECK.

ROTTERDAM IV (1908-1940) (Sterling collection)

First Class glass-enclosed promenade deck. A Holland America innovation, designed to shield against North Atlantic wind and spray whilst affording a sea view to strolling passengers. The feature proved very popular and was copied by most succeeding liners. Today's ROTTERDAM V is among the last with a walk-around partially glazed promenade deck.

T.S.S. ROTTERDAM. 24170 Tons Register. 37190 Tons Displacement.

ROTTERDAM IV (1908-1940)

(Dragonette collection)

A sepia-toned card posted from Rotterdam in August 1915. As a neutral-flag line, Holland America made enormous profits during the First World War, but the risk of mines and submarines saw ROTTERDAM IV laid up in Rotterdam from March 1916-January 1919 for safe-keeping.

HOLLAND-AMERICA LINE.　　　　　ROTTERDAM - NEW YORK

T.S.S. ROTTERDAM. 24170 Tons Register - 37190 Tons Displacement.

ROTTERDAM IV (1908-1940)   (Dragonette collection)

Another Fred Pansing card, posted upon arrival at Plymouth on 12 July 1926, reading in part: "Grand ship. Wish you were here. Fine crowd of nearly 500, by far best on all ship. Rather cold to-day and quite a swell on. Time flies..." That year ROTTERDAM IV resumed service after a major refit.

Holland-America Line. t.s.s. **ROTTERDAM**. 24149 tons register - 34740 tons displacement

ROTTERDAM IV (1908-1940)

This card was posted on ROTTERDAM IV's final long cruise, a "Summer Cruise to South America", in August 1939 for Thos. Cook & Son. After two neutral-flag trans-Atlantic crossings, ROTTERDAM IV was sold in January 1940 to Dutch breakers, a vessel whose length of service is now exceeded by the present ROTTERDAM V.

HOLLAND-AMERIKA LINIE.   ROTTERDAM - NEW YORK.

D.D. **STATENDAM.** 35000 Register Tons - 45000 Tons Wasserverdrängung.

STATENDAM II   (never sailed for H.A.L.)

Built by Harland & Wolff, Belfast. The rarest of postcards are those for vessels which never ran for their owners. A tragic example was STATENDAM II launched on 9 July 1914, but completed as the British troopship JUSTICIA (White Star Line management) in 1917. Torpedoed by U-64 on 19 July 1917 and sunk the next day by U-124. This Fred Pansing card depicts a "never to be" scene of STATENDAM II leaving Rotterdam.

TRIPLE SCREW TURBINE S. S. STATENDAM BUILDING
35000 TONS REGISTER   45000 TONS DISPLACEMENT

HOLLAND-AMERICA LINE

ROYAL DUTCH AND U. S. MAIL SERVICE

PANAMA-PACIFIC
INTERNATIONAL EXPOSITION, 1915

EXHIBIT IN PALACE OF TRANSPORTATION

PASSENGER OFFICE, 319 GEARY ST., SAN FRANCISCO, CAL.

General Passenger Office - 24 State St., New York

GENERAL PASSENGER AGENCIES

Chicago · 138 N. La Salle St.	New Orleans, 219 St. Charles St.
Boston · · · 89 State St.	Seattle · · · 108 Cherry St.
St. Louis · Locust and 11th St.	Toronto, Can., 24 Toronto St.
Minneapolis · 121 So. Third St.	Montreal, Can., 286 St. James St.

STATENDAM II
(never sailed for H.A.L.) (Maxwell collection)
Holland America still had hopes of taking delivery of STA-TENDAM II in 1915 when this card was printed to promote the line's exhibit at the Panama-Pacific International Exposition which celebrated the opening of the Panama Canal the previous year. In 1920, H.A.L. inaugurated a joint Europe-U.S. West Coast service via Panama with Britain's Royal Mail Line.

S. S. STATENDAM Holland-Amerika Lijn

STATENDAM II   (never sailed for H.A.L.) (Maxwell collection)
One of the rarest of STATENDAM II cards is this spirited broadside depiction, artist unknown. Clearly shown is the prominent extension of the superstructure forward of the bridge which was a distinguishing feature of this unfortunate vessel, the third-largest Allied ship lost in the First World War, after BRITANNIC and LUSITANIA.

HOLLAND-AMERICA LINE   ESPAÑA á CUBA y MÉJICO

9000 toneladas
de registro

Vapor „LEERDAM"

17500 toneladas
de desplazamiento

LEERDAM II (1921-1954)

Built by Nieuw Waterweg, Schiedam. 14 First 174 Second and 802 Third Class passengers. Third of a quartet of cargo-passenger liners built for H.A.L.'s Rotterdam-Cuba-Mexico service. Originally intended to be a freighter, but redesigned to carry emigrants outbound and cargo homewards, the Third Class 'tween decks convertible to cargo holds. Among the very few two-funnel "combi" ships, the after stack was a dummy.
Sister ships: MAASDAM III, EDAM IV and SPAARNDAM II

LEERDAM II (1921-1954)

Like her sister ships, powered by 4,200 shp turbines giving a service speed of 13 knots. Owing to the Depression, Cuba/Mexico passenger service withdrawn in 1932. LEERDAM II and sisters laid up. Rebuilt in in 1934 with one funnel, 30 Cabin and 60 Third Class passengers, and placed on Rotterdam-New York-Baltimore cargo-passenger service, first voyage 13 October 1934. Last voyage December 1952. 1954 broken up in Japan.

EDAM IV (1921-1954)

Built by de Schelde, Flushing. 14 First 174 Second and 800 Third Class passengers. Launched on 15 January 1921. First Rotterdam-New York-Baltimore voyage after rebuilding 14 March 1935. 30 Cabin and 60 Third Class passengers. Resumed post-war service 1946 91 First Class passengers. 1954 broken up at Hong Kong.
Sister ships: MAASDAM III, LEERDAM II and SPAARNDAM II

SPAARNDAM II (1922-1939) (Watson collection)

Built by Nieuw Waterweg, Schiedam. 14 First 174 Second and 800 Third Class passengers. Launched 11 January 1922 and laid up after only nine years on the Cuba/Mexico run for which this Spanish postcard was printed. Rebuilt for New York service, first voyage 23 October 1935. First H.A.L. loss in Second World War when sunk by magnetic mine at mouth of River Thames, 27 November 1939. Five dead.
Sister ships: MAASDAM III, EDAM IV and LEERDAM II

BLOMMERSDYK II (1922-1957)

Built by Giessen & Zonen, Krimpen a/d Ijssel. One of eight "B"-class ships and only one to survive Second World War. Typical of H.A.L. freighters, all with names ending with -DYK. BLOMMERSDYK II, like most of them, had a few passenger berths, in her case three, raised in 1934 to seven. 22 February 1957 sold to Soc. di Nav. Jonica Catania, renamed VIVARA. 1960 scrapped.

Sister ships: BURGERDYK, BLIJDENDYK, BINNENDYK, BILDERDYK, BOSCHDYK, BREEDYK and BEEMSTERDYK.

D.D. **VOLENDAM.** 15434 Register Tons 25400 Tons Wasserverdrängung.

VOLENDAM I (1922-1951)

Built by Harland & Wolff, Govan. 263 First 436 Second 1,200 Third Class passengers. VOLENDAM I and VEENDAM II, laid down for the I.M.M. "Pool" lines before the First World War, were bought on the stocks by H.A.L. VOLENDAM I was launched on 6 July 1922 after two unsuccessful attempts. The best looking of the "REGINA-class" (REGINA, PITTSBURGH, DORIC and LAURENTIC), the "V"s were among H.A.L.'s most popular and successful ships. Sister ship: VEENDAM II

T.S.S. VOLENDAM. 15430 TONS REGISTER - 25620 TONS DISPLACEMENT.

VOLENDAM I (1922-1951)   (Sterling collection)

Evacuating 335 British children to Canada, VOLENDAM I was torpedoed 30 August 1940 by a German U-boat 200 miles off Bloody Foreland, Ireland (1 dead), beached on Isle of Bute, repaired and resumed transport service after 10 months. Carried over 100,000 troops in the Second World War.

VOLENDAM I (1922-1951)

Never restored to commercial H.A.L. service post-war, she carried Dutch troops to Indonesia and emigrants to Australia and Canada. Also made some student voyages from the U.S.A. to Europe. This postcard dates from that service. 13 November 1951 sold to NV Frank Rijsdijk, Henrick-Ido-Ambacht, for scrap.

T.S.S. **VEENDAM**. 15450 Tons Register - 25600 Tons Displacement.

VEENDAM II (1923-1953)

Built by Harland & Wolff, Govan. 262 First 436 Second 1,200 Third Class passengers. January 1930 bridge smashed by freak wave in North Atlantic. Chartered summer 1931 to Furness Withy for New York-Bermuda cruise service as replacement for burnt-out BERMUDA.
Sister ship: VOLENDAM I

HOLLAND-AMERICA LINE

3ᴿᴰ CLASS CABIN.

THIRD CLASS BILL OF FARE

S. S. „Veendam" May 30th 1926

BREAKFAST

Fresh Fruit
Oatmeal
Fried Eggs
Graham and White Bread   Butter
Cold Meat   Jam
Coffee

DINNER

Rice Soup
Roast Quarter of Mutton
Mixed French Beans   Boiled Potatoes
Graham and White Bread   Butter
Ice-Cream
Coffee

SUPPER

Swedish salad
Haché of Beef
Graham and White Bread   Butter
Cheese   Jam
Tea

3 P.M. Coffee or Tea, Biscuits

VEENDAM II (1923-1953)   (Dragonette collection)

A most unusual postcard of a Third Class menu card aboard VEENDAM I 30 May 1926. They even "dressed" for dinner in Third Class then! Note the washbasin with single (cold) faucet, four berths and spartan painted wooden bulkheads. The bill of fare, featuring roast mutton and boiled potatoes, a far cry from today's lavish H.A.L. dining, is also typical for this class.

Holland-America Line. t.s.s. **VEENDAM.** 15450 tons register - 25620 tons displacement

VEENDAM II (1923-1953)

In September 1939 VEENDAM II rescued survivors of torpedoed aircraft carrier H.M.S. COURAGEOUS in North Atlantic. Left New York for Rotterdam on 30 March 1940 and was captured intact at Rotterdam in May 1940. Used by the Germans as a submarine tender at Gotenhaven (Gdynia), Poland, and later moved to Hamburg where she was damaged by Allied bombing.

VEENDAM II (1923-1953)

Returned to H.A.L. in October 1945 and refitted for 223 First and 363 Tourist passengers. Resumed Rotterdam-New York service 21 December 1947. Popular to the end, this 1952 card reads: "Boat trip over was simply marvelous. Didn't want to leave. Very smooth all the way. Food was excellent. Service wonderful." 30 October 1953 sold to Bethlehem Steel and broken up at Baltimore, USA.

T.S.S. **STATENDAM**. 28291 Tons Register - 38950 Tons Displacement.

STATENDAM III (1929-1940)

Built by Harland & Wolff, Belfast. 510 First 344 Second 374 Tourist and 426 Third Class passengers. "Queen of the Spotless Fleet" and last of the Edwardian-style liners, STATENDAM III was laid down in June 1921, launched on 11 September 1924, towed to Schiedam in 1927 for completion by Wilton-Fijenoord, and did not make her maiden voyage until 11 April 1929—an eight-year crawl to a career of only 11 years.

S.S. Statendam. H.A.L.

(Maxwell collection)

STATENDAM III (1929-1940)

Similar to the ill-fated STATENDAM II, the 1929-built ship had a cruiser stern and no superstructure extension forward. Good for 19 knots and fitted with six superheated watertube boilers, she was renowned for her economical operation. Leaving New York for "safekeeping" in Rotterdam on 9 December 1939, the ship's end was cruelly ironic. Caught in a crossfire between German and Dutch forces, she was burnt out 11-12 May 1940 and scrapped in August.

STATENDAM III (1929-1940) (Dragonette collection)
First Class lounge, from a series of interior postcards sold in the ship's shop. The last traditionally decorated trans-Atlantic liner for the Northern Europe-New York route, STATENDAM III was famous for her lavish interiors. The two-storey lounge was panelled in oak, furnished with Louis XIV style chairs and decorated with Gobelin tapestries and period paintings.

STATENDAM III (1929-1940)　　　　　　　　　　　　　　　　　　　　　　　　(Dragonette collection

First Class smoking room. Although lady visitors were indulged by the twenties, the liner smoking room retained masculine
comfort and decor, here featuring a Flemish character and the typical stuffed leather armchairs round a working fireplace.

STATENDAM III (1929-1940)

First Class dining room. Seating 400, this two-storey room was decorated in Louis XVI style with a magnificent painted ceiling. Thick carpeting, upholstered armchairs, fine linen and company monogrammed silver service provided an elegant accompaniment to some of the finest cuisine on the North Atlantic run.

STATENDAM III (1929-1940)
First Class swimming pool. This was the first H.A.L. liner with a permanent indoor pool, a fanciful confection of glazed tiles. The glass-smooth surface of the water and the slight list indicate this photo was taken at pierside. On warm-weather cruises, an outdoor canvas pool was rigged on deck.

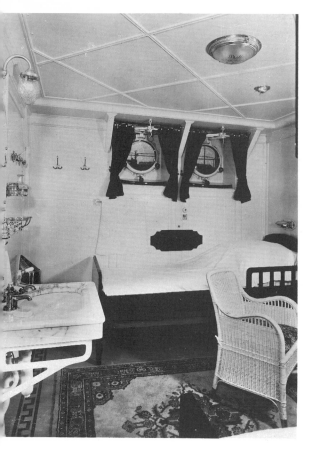

STATENDAM III (1929-1940)   (Sterling collection)
First Class stateroom. Commodious and comfortable cabins
have been a Holland America hallmark since ROT-
TERDAM IV of 1908. This STATENDAM III accommodation features a marble-topped washbasin, two
portholes, wicker easy chair and an oriental carpet. In 1937,
you could take an eight-day New York-Nassau cruise for $90
and up.

STATENDAM III (1929-1940)   (Dragonette collection)
"Having a great time, wish you were here"? Yes H.A.L.
even issued a bathroom postcard! STATENDAM III had
the highest proportion of private-bath cabins of any trans
Atlantic liner of her day. This lavish facility, complete with
bidet, includes tub taps for both fresh and salt water. The
line was the first to have all-facility cabins in First Class
(NIEUW AMSTERDAM II 1938) and in all cabins
(NOORDAM II 1938).

HOLLAND · AMERICA LINE
PACIFIC COAST *via* PANAMA CANAL *to* EUROPE

Twin-Screw Diesel M. S. DELFTDYK and DAMSTERDYK

10,220 tons gross register   Length — 510 feet   20,675 tons displacement

D-4279

DELFTDYK/DONGEDYK (1929-1966)   (Watson collection)

Built by Wilton, Schiedam, as DELFTDYK for the Rotterdam-Vancouver cargo-passenger service. 30 Cabin Class passengers. After DINTELDYK I (1922) and DRECHTDYK (1923) introduced diesel-propulsion to H.A.L., two further "D's" were built for the trans-Panama route. 10 May 1940 bombed off Flushing and again at Peterhead in September 1941, out of service for a year.
Sister ship: DAMSTERDYK/DALERDYK

DELFTDYK/DONGEDYK (1929-1966)   (Watson collection)

January 1950 damaged by mine at mouth of Weser. Resumed service as DONGEDYK in 1952 with new engines, funnel, bridge and bows. June 1966 to Toshin Trading Co., Kobe, renamed TUNG LONG for voyage to Kaohsiung for breaking. In a scene repeated weekly in summer by the present H.A.L. Alaskan cruising fleet, DONGEDYK passes under Vancouver Lion Gate Bridge.

DAMSTERDYK/DALERDYK (1930-1963)

Built by Harland & Wolff, Govan, as DAMSTERDYK for the Rotterdam-Vancouver service. 30 Cabin Class passengers. Seized by Germany during the Second World War. 28 January 1949 renamed DALERDYK and resumed service after extensive refit by Wilton-Fijenoord including new engines, funnel and bridge (as shown in this card). Sister ship: DELFTDYK/DONGEDYK

DAMSTERDYK/DALERDYK (1930-1963)

Labelled as DALERDYK, this card actually depicts DONGEDYK (distinguished by her raked bow and forward set of kingposts) passing through the Panama Canal, always a highlight for passengers. 26 July 1963 to Belvientos Cie. Nav. SA Panama, renamed PRESVIA. August 1963 to Japanese breakers.

T.S.S. **NIEUW AMSTERDAM.** 33000 TONS REGISTER — MAIDEN TRIP MAY 1938.

NIEUW AMSTERDAM II (1938-1973)

A pre-maiden voyage card of this remarkable vessel, the second-largest liner ever built in the Netherlands. The building of Holland's "Ship of State" was an act of national faith. Dutch Government loans and pay cuts offered by shipyard workers facilitated her construction during the Depression.

S/S NEW AMSTERDAM STEAMING UP THE HUDSON

NIEUW AMSTERDAM II (1938-1973) (Dragonette collection)

Built by Rotterdamsche Droogdok, Rotterdam. 556 Cabin 455 Tourist 209 Third Class passengers. Laid down on 3 January 1936 with the proposed name PRINSENDAM and launched on 10 April 1937 by Queen Wilhelmina. Powered by 34,000 shp single-reduction geared turbines, the 20.5-knot NIEUW AMSTERDAM was then the largest twin-screw liner in the world.

NIEUW AMSTERDAM II (1938-1973)

(Sterling collection)

Arriving at New York on her maiden voyage, 16 May 1938, from Rotterdam, Boulogne-sur-Mer and Southampton. She quickly joined the elite "Ships of State", QUEEN MARY, NORMANDIE, BREMEN, EUROPA and REX, as the Atlantic run reached its pre-war pinnacle.

S.S. NIEUW AMSTERDAM 36,667 TONS
FLAGSHIP OF THE
Holland-America Line

NIEUW AMSTERDAM II (1938-1973)

NIEUW AMSTERDAM II passing the Hook of Holland. Hers was the perfect 'thirties liner profile and few ships boasted such handsome, pleasing lines. Smaller and slower than the "superliners", she was no less luxurious and popular, and considerably more profitable.

s.s. NIEUW AMSTERDAM der Holland-Amerika Lijn

KLM.Foto-Copyright 15508

NIEUW AMSTERDAM II (1938-1973)

(Maxwell collection)

A superb aerial photo card by KLM showing the ship's extensive unobstructed open deck space, the solarium behind the bridge and the forward working funnel and the dummy aft one.

S. S. Nieuw Amsterdam

NIEUW AMSTERDAM II (1938-1973)

Last leaving Rotterdam on 22 September 1939, NIEUW AMSTERDAM II made a triumphant return on 10 April 1946 after having steamed 530,452 miles and carrying 378,361 wartime passengers, including the entire Royal Family of Greece. Resumed service after extensive refit on 29 October 1947.

NIEUW AMSTERDAM II (1938-1973)
(Sterling collection)

First Class dining saloon. Designed to connect with the similarly decorated Cabin Class saloon (aft) on cruises, this was originally, with the theatre, the only air-conditioned public room in the ship. Very much the national flagship, every room was lavished with the creations of Dutch artists, artisans and architects.

NIEUW AMSTERDAM II (1938-1973)

In 1957, the hull was repainted dove grey with a gold sheer line and air-conditioning extended throughout ship. A further refit in 1961 re-arranged accommodation to 574 First and 583 Tourist Class passengers. This 1957 card reads in part: "So far it is calm, but not much sun today—Sunday. My cabin is comfortable, but small!"

ADVERTISING CARD c. 1880s   (Dragonette collection)
This charming card, in German, depicts the company houseflag—the green and white colours (those of the City of Rotterdam) and the initials N.A.S.M. for Nederlandsche-Amerikaansche Stoomvaart Maatschappij or the Netherlands American Steamship Line. Operations had already commenced under the Plate, Reuchin & Co. name with the voyage of ROTTERDAM I from Flushing to New York, 15 October-5 November 1872, with 10 saloon and 60 steerage passengers aboard.

HOLLAND-AMERIKA LINIE.   ROTTERDAM - NEW YORK.

D.D. **NOORDAM.** 12531 Register Tons - 22070 Tons Wasserverdrängung.

NOORDAM I (1902-1927)

One of the few trans-Atlantic liners to maintain regular sailings during the First World War. At a cost, however, as NOORDAM I was damaged twice by mines in the North Sea in October 1914 and August 1917. Laid up until 1919 and then resumed service.

D.D. **NIEUW-AMSTERDAM.** 17250 Register Tons - **31000** Tons Wasserverdrängung.

NIEUW AMSTERDAM I (1906-1932)

Posted from New York on 26 July 1915, this card depicts the vessel after her forward promenade was glass enclosed in 1908 and her superstructure extended forward the next year. On 21 December 1918 NIEUW AMSTERDAM I resumed H.A.L. sailings shortly after the Armistice. 26 February 1932 left Rotterdam for Osaka and breaking up.

T.S.S. **ROTTERDAM.** 24150 Tons Register - 34740 Tons Displacement.

ROTTERDAM IV (1908-1940)

Perhaps the best of the series of cards done by Charles Dixon in 1925. Posted at Funchal, Madeira, in February 1932 on one of the ship's many cruises—"Lots to do every minute between dances in evening, horse races, holiday celebrations, tournaments, deck games etc." Holland America was among the first lines with cruise directors to keep passengers entertained.

D.D. **VEENDAM.** 15450 REGISTER TONS - 25600 TONS WASSERVERDRÄNGUNG.

VEENDAM II (1923-1953)

Maritime painter Charles Dixon, indulging in artistic license, has portrayed smoke coming from both funnels when, in fact, the second one on both "V"s was a dummy used to ventilate the engine room. A twin-screw turbine steamer, VEENDAM II had a service speed of 15 knots.

Holland-America Line. t.s.s. **NIEUW AMSTERDAM.** 36287 tons register - 36235 tons displacement

NIEUW AMSTERDAM II (1938-1973)

This postcard reproduction of the classic Frank H. Mason painting was mailed from Punta Arenas, Chile, on 4 March 1939, on the liner's first long cruise, round South America. Upon the outbreak of war, she operated neutral-flag cruises. When Holland was invaded in May 1940, she was made available to the Allies and converted into a transport (capacity 8,000 troops) at Halifax.

Holland America Cruises

s.s. Veendam-s.s. Volendam

VOLENDAM II & VEENDAM III (1972-1983)

Built in 1958 by Ingalls, Pascagoula, Miss., USA, as BRASIL and ARGENTINA for Moore-McCormack Lines, N.Y.-S. America service. April 1971 to H.A.L., refitted at Bremerhaven, 700 one-class passengers. Acquired for new worldwide de luxe cruising, the "V"s had all new public rooms and retained their spacious original staterooms. Funnel is a dummy with twin uptakes aft.

STATENDAM V (1993-present)

The first of three elegant liners, STATENDAM V was christened at Port Canaveral by Mrs. Lin Arison, wife of Carnival Cruise Lines' founder Ted Arison. 1266 passengers are accommodated over 10 decks and the attractive decor includes US$2 million of Dutch art treasures and artifacts, maintaining a tradition started in 1938 with the most modern entertainment facilities. STATENDAM V commenced her maiden voyage, a 16 day cruise to California via Panama, on 23 January 1993.
Sister ships: MAASDAM V, RYNDAM III

Holland America Cruises

s.s. Nieuw Amsterdam

NIEUW AMSTERDAM II (1938-1973)

NIEUW AMSTERDAM II was re-boilered in 1967 and left Rotterdam on 8 November 1971 on H.A.L.'s final trans-Atlantic crossing. Thereafter based on Port Everglades for Caribbean cruising. Last cruise December 1973. 2 March 1974 arrived Kaohsiung for breaking up. This is her last postcard, printed in 1973, H.A.L.'s 100th anniversary.

Holland-America Line m.v. "NOORDAM"

NOORDAM II (1938-1963)

Built by P. Smit, Rotterdam. 160 Tourist Class passengers. NOORDAM II's maiden voyage in September 1938 marked a new era in trans-Atlantic travel: the "combi" liner combining de luxe one-class accommodation (all but one cabin outside and all with private facilities, the first on the Atlantic) and substantial cargo capacity. A pre-maiden voyage card by Frank H. Mason.
Sister ship: ZAANDAM II

NOORDAM II (1938-1963)

Transferred with ZAANDAM II (torpedoed off Brazil 1942) in February-March 1940 to a new New York-Java via the Cape service. 1942-1945 served as U.S. troopship. July 1946 resumed Rotterdam-New York run. May 1963 to Cielomar SA, Panama, chartered to Messageries Maritimes as OCEANIEN Marseilles-Sydney service. 1967 scrapped at Split, Yugoslavia.

Holland-America Line s.s. "Westernland"

WESTERNLAND (1939-1942) (Maxwell collection)

Built 1918 by Harland & Wolff, Belfast, as REGINA (Dominion Line), December 1925 to White Star Line. 1929 WESTERNLAND (Red Star Line), 1935 to Bernstein Red Star and June 1939 to H.A.L., same name and service, Antwerp-New York. 486 Tourist Class passengers. A rare H.A.L.-issued card showing vessel still in Red Star Line colours. Sister ship: PENNLAND

s.s. „VEENDAM"
Holland-Amerika Lijn

WESTERNLAND/PENNLAND   (Maxwell collection)

Although labelled as VEENDAM, this card actually depicts WESTERNLAND/PENNLAND clearly distinguished from the related "V" ships by the separate bridge structure. As the vessel was only in H.A.L. service June 1939-April 1940, such cards are indeed a rarity. WESTERNLAND was sold to the British Admiralty in November 1942, converted into a repair ship and scrapped at Blyth in August 1947. PENNLAND was sunk 25 April 1941 by the Luftwaffe in the Gulf of Athens.

Holland-America Line M.V. Sommelsdyk and Sloterdyk

SOMMELSDYK III (1939-1965) (Dragonette collection)

Built by A.P. Moller, Odense, for H.A.L.'s New York-Java via Cape Town service. 12 Cabin Class passengers. August 1942 converted into U.S. transport. Christmas Day 1944 hit by aerial torpedo in Leyte Gulf, causing 30 ft. x 20 ft. hole, repaired. 9 May 1946 returned to Netherlands Government and chartered to H.A.L. after refit. 4 June 1965 sold for scrap to Castelon, Spain, breakers.
Sister ship: SLOTERDYK II

SLOTERDYK II (1940-1966)   (Dragonette collection)

Built by A.P. Moller, Odense, for New York-Java service. 12 Cabin Class passengers. 1942 converted into U.S. transport (1,666 troops). 21 February 1946 returned to Netherlands Government and chartered to H.A.L. 1948. 3 May 1966 sold for scrap to Alicante, Spain, breakers. This post-war card still shows ship with wartime liferafts.
Sister ship: SOMMELSDYK III

WESTERDAM I (1946-1964)

Built by Wilton-Fijenoord, Schiedam. 134 First Class passengers. Laid down the day Germany invaded Poland, launched on 27 July 1940, sunk by Allied bombing on 27 August 1942 and again by Dutch underground in September 1944. Raised and completed, her maiden voyage Rotterdam-New York 28 June 1946 was the first for a new liner after war and first postwar H.A.L. crossing. Last voyage October 1964. 1965 scrapped at Alicante.
Sister ships: ZUIDERDAM (never completed)

ANDYK II (1946-1969) (Maxwell collection)

Built by Sun, Chester, USA, as C3-class GRONIGEN for Netherlands Government (handed over 7 October 1946), chartered to H.A.L. and renamed ANDYK II. 12 Cabin Class passengers. Rotterdam-Mexico/Gulf ports service. 5 September 1969 to Sandra Shipping Co. (Cyprus), renamed AURORA. 8 May 1971 arrived Castellon, Spain, for breaking up.

EEMDYK III (1946-1960) (Dragonette collection)

Built in 1944 by Caledon, Dundee, as EMPIRE ALBION (UK Government). 23 May 1944 to Netherlands Government, renamed TERBORCH. 10 October 1946 to H.A.L., renamed EEMDYK III. 12 Cabin Class passengers. Rotterdam-Mexico/Gulf ports service. 6 April 1960 to Labrador Cia. Nav. SA (Monrovia), renamed ZAMBESI. 19 November 1967 to Kaohsiung breakers.

DUIVENDYK (1946-1959)   (Watson collection)

Built in 1930 by Deutsche Werft, Hamburg, as VANCOUVER for Hamburg America Line. May 1940 seized by Dutch Navy in West Indies, operated by KNSM as CURACAO. 3 July 1946 to H.A.L., renamed DUIVENDYK, 30 Cabin Class passengers. Rotterdam-Vancouver service. 28 July 1959 to Chung Hing Enterprise, Hong Kong, for scrap.

AVERDYK (1947-1967)

Built in 1944 by California Shipbuilding, Los Angeles, USA, as DURHAM VICTORY. 29 January 1947 to Netherlands Government and chartered to H.A.L. The third of 13 VC2-type wartime Victory ships for the line, the largest class ever operated by H.A.L. and backbone of the cargo operations into the 'sixties. 10 May 1967 to Consolidated Mariners (Panama) as DOMINA. December 1971 scrapped at Kaohsiung.

Sister ships: AMSTELDYK, ARKELDYK, AALSDYK, ABBEDYK, AXELDYK, AARDYK, ARNEDYK, ARENDSDYK, AKKRUMDYK, AAGTEDYK and APPINGEDYK.

ALMDYK (1948-1965)

Built by Ingalls, Pascagoula, USA as converted C3-class escort aircraft carrier USS BLOCK ISLAND, 1942. 1948 rebuilt into a C3-class freighter by Gulf Shipbuilding, Mobile. 17 November 1948 to Netherlands Government, chartered to H.A.L., renamed ALMDYK. 12 Cabin Class passengers. Rotterdam-Mexico/Gulf ports service. 27 October 1965 sold for scrap, Castellon, Spain.

SOESTDYK II (1948-1967)

Built by Harland & Wolff, Belfast. 12 Cabin Class passengers. First H.A.L. freighter with automatic hatch covers. New York-Java run. 1960 rebuilt at Wilton-Fijenoord into an open shelter-deck ship and re-engined with Sulzer diesels instead of steam turbines. Antwerp-New York (Red Star Line) service. 1970 sold to Soc. di Nav., Palermo, and renamed LORENZO D'AMICO. Scrapped in Taiwan in 1978.
Sister ship: SCHIEDYK II

SCHIEDYK II (1949-1968)

Last in a long line of H.A.L. ships built by Harland & Wolff, Belfast. 12 Cabin Class passengers. New York-Java run. 1960 rebuilt and re-engined like sister ship at Wilton-Fijenoord. Antwerp-New York (Red Star Line) service. 4 January 1968 aground in Zuciarte Channel near Bligh Island and lost.
Sister ship: SOESTDYK II

DIEMERDYK (1950-1968)

Built by Wilton-Fijenoord, Schiedam, for Rotterdam-Vancouver service. 61 Cabin Class passengers. First newly built ship in the Netherlands after the war. Luxurious cargo-passenger liner with 32 all outside, air-conditioned cabins and full range of public rooms. Like MAASDAM/RYNDAM (q.v.) powered by U.S.-built war surplus General Electric turbines. Sister ship: DINTELDYK

DIEMERDYK (1950-1968)

Shown here at San Francisco with one of the Matson Line Hawaii liners at her berth in the background. 3 December 1968 to Oriental Africa Lines (Liberia) for C.Y. Tung's round the world service, renamed ORIENTAL AMIGA. January 1980 scrapped at Kaohsiung.

GROOTE BEER (1951-1963)

Built in 1944 by Permanente Metals, Richmond, California, USA, as Victory type COSTA RICA VICTORY. 1947 to Nederland Line, converted into emigrant ship (900 berths) GROOTE BEER. 1951 H.A.L. management. Voyages to North America, Australia and South Africa. 1963 to Latsis, Greece, MARIANNA IV, rechartered by H.A.L. 1965-6 for student voyages as GROOTE BEER. June 1970 scrapped at Eleusis, Greece.

RYNDAM II (1951-1972)

Built by Wilton-Fijenoord, Schiedam. Laid down in 1949 as DINTELDYK II, sister ship to DIEMERDYK (q.v.). Redesigned as a liner and launched in December 1950 as RYNDAM II. 39 First and 842 Tourist Class passengers. One of the most influential liners ever built, giving Tourist Class run of the ship with new standards for budget travellers. First all air-conditioned liner on Channel ports-New York run.
Sister ship: MAASDAM IV

RYNDAM II (1951-1972)

This card, mailed in 1959, reads: "I want to thank you for arranging my very comfortable outside cabin & as no body else came to settle in it, I'm in cozy seclusion. The bulletin says "heavy sea" & "moderate swell" but I am still on deck! As you said, the ship is an excellent one." The next year RYNDAM II began a new Rotterdam-Montreal service during summer months.

RYNDAM II (1951-1972) (Sterling collection)

In addition to her novel accommodation, RYNDAM II introduced the new dove grey hull scheme for Holland America and was the first Atlantic liner with the Strombus aerofoil-type funnel, designed to prevent smuts from falling on deck.

RYNDAM II (1951-1972)

(Watson collection)

RYNDAM II was transferred in 1966 to subsidiary German company, Europa-Kanada Linie, in whose colours she is shown in this rare card. Returned to Dutch flag as WATERMAN, then RYNDAM II before being sold in 1972 to Epirotiki Cruises. Converted to cruise ship ATLAS. 1989 to Pride Cruise Lines, renamed PRIDE OF MISSISSIPPI for day cruises from Galveston, later renamed PRIDE OF GALVESTON and laid up in 1991.

MAASDAM IV (1952-1968) (Sterling collection)

Built by Wilton-Fijenoord, Schiedam. 39 First and 842 Tourist Class passengers. August 1952 maiden voyage Rotterdam-New York via Montreal. This photo was taken from the passing RYNDAM II. On maiden call at Bremerhaven in February 1963 damaged in collision with two submerged wrecks. Passengers evacuated in lifeboats, ship later repaired. Sister ship: RYNDAM II

MAASDAM IV (1952-1968) (Sterling collection)

The "Economy Twins" could roll and pitch terribly and in 1955 MAASDAM IV became the first H.A.L. vessel fitted with Denny Brown stabilizers. Even so, this card, posted from Nassau in 1957 on one of her many cruises, reads: "So far the weather is gorgeous, even so there's quite a roll. Pills in much demand."

MAASDAM IV (1952-1968)

Ran Rotterdam-Montreal 1966 onwards. 1968 to Polish Ocean Lines, renamed STEFAN BATORY. Uniquely, continued old H.A.L. route, adding Gdynia, Poland. Last traditional trans-Atlantic liner and the last to serve Canada and call at Rotterdam. The ever-popular ship was withdrawn in 1987 and sold to Stena Line. Presently an accommodation vessel in Sweden.

SEVEN SEAS (1955-1966)

Built in 1940 by Sun Shipbuilding, Chester, Pennsylvania, USA, as C3 type freighter MORMACMAIL. 1941 rebuilt as aircraft carrier USS LONG ISLAND. 1948 converted into emigrant ship NELLIE. 1953 SEVEN SEAS 20 First and 987 Tourist Class passengers. 1955 to Europa-Kanada Linie, a H.A.L. subsidiary. Maintained regular Bremerhaven-Montreal sailings.

SEVEN SEAS (1955-1966)

(Sterling collection)

This card depicts a typical sailing scene—for emigrants, the ship was the start of a new life in North America or Australia and in reverse direction, she carried many students and budget tourists on their first trip to Europe. 1966 replaced by RYNDAM II (q.v.) and became accommodation ship at Rotterdam. May 1977 scrapped in Belgium.

KINDERDYK II (1956-1970)

Built by De Schelde, Flushing. 12 Cabin Class passengers. First of a new "K" class of freighters, among the best-looking operated by H.A.L. Note: only KINDERDYK II and KLOOSTERDYK had passenger accommodation. Antwerp-New York (Red Star Line) service. April 1970 to Splosna Plovba Piran, Yugoslavia, renamed BOROVNICA. December 1982 scrapped at Split.
Sister ships: KLOOSTERDYK, KERKEDYK, KAMPERDYK, KORENDYK and KASTEDYK.

KLOOSTERDYK (1957-1970)   (Watson collection)

Built by Jan Smit, Amsterdam. 12 Cabin Class passengers. The second of the "K" class and the last passenger carrying freighter built for H.A.L. Antwerp-New York (Red Star Line) service. March 1970 to Splosna Plovba Piran, Yugoslavia, renamed BREZICE. 1982 to Maroa Lines (Honduras), renamed MAROU VII.
Sister ships: KINDERDYK II, KERKEDYK, KAMPERDYK, KORENDYK and KATSEDYK.

S.S. STATENDAM, *HOLLAND-AMERICA LINE*
24,294 GROSS TONS   LENGTH 642 FT 3 INS.   BEAM 78 FT 9 INS.   SERVICE SPEED 19 KNOTS

STATENDAM IV (1957-1981)

(Maxwell collection)

Built by Wilton-Fijenoord, Schiedam. 84 First and 847 Tourist Class passengers. Built in a graving dock and floated out on 12 June 1956 with official christening, by Princess Beatrix (now H.M. The Queen), taking place on trials in January 1957. First Atlantic crossing from Rotterdam 6 February concluded at New York during a tugboat strike and the ship successfully docked unaided.

STATENDAM IV (1957-1981) (Sterling collection)

An evocative photo card of STATENDAM IV at night alongside H.A.L.'s Wilhelminakade pier and headquarters, Rotterdam. This landmark structure still stands, although vacant and with an uncertain future. It originally included a special hotel to accommodate emigrants sailing for America in H.A.L. ships.

STATENDAM IV (1957-1981)

A dramatic card of H.A.L.'s best-looking post-war liner. Basically an improved RYNDAM II with greater speed (19 knots), increased First Class and enhanced Tourist, 90 per cent with private facilities. The first company ship built with stabilizers and with a permanent outside swimming pool.

STATENDAM IV (1957-1981)

STATENDAM IV transits the Panama Canal on a cruise. Ideal in size and accommodation for the purpose, she was employed exclusively as a cruise ship from 1966 onwards, including H.A.L.'s first cruise programme from the U.S. West Coast. Made the first round the world cruise for H.A.L. in 1958.

STATENDAM IV (1957-1981) (Dragonette collection)
The Tourist Class Ocean Bar. STATENDAM IV had the most *avant garde* decor of any post-war H.A.L. ship and her Tourist Class was quite the most luxurious of its day.

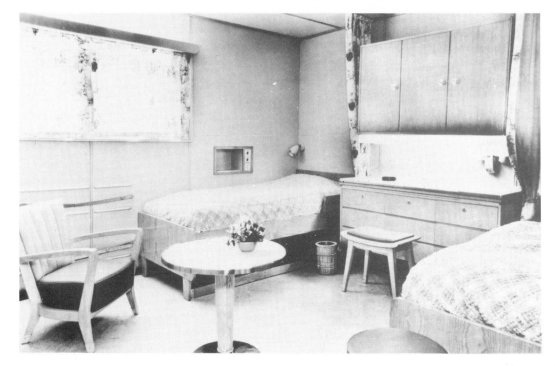

STATENDAM IV (1957-1981)

Tourist Class stateroom. The ship introduced a new standard for budget travel and this roomy, twin-bedded cabin is typical. Note the lavish drawer and cupboard space, armchair and table. So successful was this design that it was carried over in ROTTERDAM V two years later.

STATENDAM IV (1957-1981)

Main engine control station. Engine room postcards are obviously a rarity, this one from a set of cards sold in the ship's shop. STATENDAM IV was a twin-screw ship, powered by the newest type of turbines, 22,000 shp cross-compound Pametradas supplied by two high-pressure Foster-Wheeler boilers. The ship often proved mechanically troublesome, especially in her later years.

Holland America Cruises   The luxurious s.s. STATENDAM

STATENDAM IV (1957-1981)

From September 1971-February 1972 STATENDAM IV was rebuilt for cruising, including new boilers and an entirely new Promenade Deck. She introduced a new livery of midnight blue hull and orange funnel with aqua green-white-aqua green "flash" logo. Sold October 1981 to Paquet Cruises, renamed RHAPSODY. 1985 sold to Regency Cruises, re-engined with diesels and renamed REGENT STAR. Presently in service.

DINTELDYK II (1957-1970)

Built by Wilton-Fijenoord, Schiedam, for Rotterdam-Vancouver service. Completed seven years after DIEMERDYK (q.v.), her double bottom was built by Cockerill, Antwerp, and towed to Schiedam for completion. Ended H.A.L. Vancouver run and sold June 1970 to Orient Overseas Lines (Liberia), renamed ORIENTAL FANTASIA. March 1979 scrapped at Kaohsiung as HONG KONG SUCCESS.

Sister ship: DIEMERDYK (differs by having raked funnel)

S.S. ROTTERDAM, *HOLLAND-AMERICA LINE*
37,000 GROSS TONS.   LENGTH 748 FT.   BEAM 94 FT.   SERVICE SPEED 21½ KNOTS

ROTTERDAM V (1959- present)

Built by Rotterdamsche Droogdok, Rotterdam. 647 First and 809 Tourist Class. Flagship of H.A.L. for more than 30 years, largest liner ever built in the Netherlands and one of the most beloved ships of the post-war era. A pre-maiden voyage illustration by C.A. Garman.

ROTTERDAM V (1959- present)

A ship with a royal beginning: launched by Queen Juliana on 13 September 1958, Her Majesty also commissioned the vessel on 22 August 1959. Princess Beatrix sailed on the maiden voyage to New York 3-11 September 1959, coinciding with the 350th anniversary of the founding of Nieuw Amsterdam (New York). This card shows Princess Beatrix embarking on the Dutch warship GELDERLAND in New York Harbor.

NEW YORK HARBOR

ROTTERDAM V (1959- present)   (Sterling collection)
Maiden arrival at New York, showing her unique profile. Nowadays considered a "classic" liner, her design was very forward-looking in 1959; first Atlantic liner without conventional funnels, "horizontal" class division and easily convertible to cruising.

ROTTERDAM V (1959-present)   (Dragonette collection)

Another maiden arrival card, an aerial view showing her extensive tiered open decks, twin uptakes and midships passenger observation deck. Like STATENDAM IV she has an outdoor pool (originally for Tourist Class) as well as indoor one (for First).

ROTTERDAM V (1959- present) (Dragonette collection)

Tourist Class "La Fontaine" dining room. Although each class had its own separate decks and facilities, the decor of the public rooms was comparable and of all the sixties "superliners", ROTTERDAM was the easiest to convert to one-class cruising. Her first cruise was in December 1959, 49 days round South America, followed by the first annual world cruise in February 1960.

ROTTERDAM V (1959- present)   (Sterling collection)

"Lynbaan" Shopping Centre. ROTTERDAM had the most extensive shopping areas of any liner of her day and the "Lynbaan", named after the City of Rotterdam's main shopping street, remains unchanged except for the addition of carpeting and, alas the prices are no longer vintage 1959!

ROTTERDAM V (1959- present)

Powerful yet elegant-looking in her original dove grey hull, ROTTERDAM V at speed—at 20 knots, she burns 195 tons of heavy oil a day. Far more economical than other trans-Atlantic liners of the era, she is fitted with 35,000 shp Schelde-Parson turbines, four boilers and twin screws. Few liners have enjoyed as mechanically troublefree a career.

Holland America Cruises

Deluxe Flagship ROTTERDAM

ROTTERDAM V (1959- present)

During its 100th anniversary 1973, H.A.L. restyled itself as Holland America Cruises, repainted ROTTERDAM V in the new midnight blue hull colours and based her at New York for seven-day Bermuda-Nassau summer cruises. Ten years later, she transferred to Alaska cruises from Vancouver.

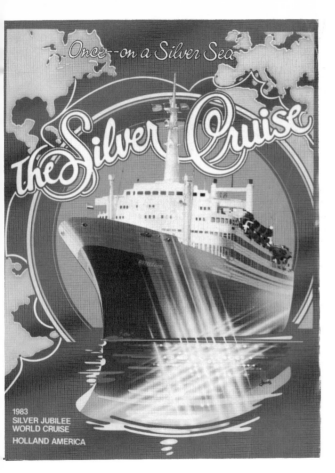

Once--on a Silver Sea

The Silver Cruise

1983
SILVER JUBILEE
WORLD CRUISE
HOLLAND AMERICA

ROTTERDAM V (1959- present)
(Maxwell collection)

A special commemorative postcard issued for "The Silver Jubilee World Cruise", the 25th such voyage made by ROTTERDAM V. Due to world conditions, the last such trip was made three years later, but in 1990 she resumed long distance voyaging with a Grand Circle South America Cruise. In 1992 she again cruised round the world. Long may cruising's "Grande Dame" sail on!

PRINSES MARGRIET (1964-1970)

Built by "De Merwede", Hardinxveld/Giessendam for Oranje Lijn, 1961. 111 First Class passengers. 10 November 1964 to H.A.L. (made four voyages under charter in 1963) for Rotterdam-New York service, replacing NOORDAM II (q.v.). December 1967 final voyage. 1968 chartered to KNSM. 1970 to Republic of Nauru, renamed ENNA G. Laid up in 1983. Arrived Thap Sakae, Thailand, for scrapping 8 September 1990.

POELDYK II (1964-1974)

Built by August Pahl, Hamburg. Eight Cabin Class passengers. Rotterdam-Mexico/Gulf ports service. A one-off ship, purchased on the stocks by H.A.L. January 1973 to H.A.L. subsidiary Trans-Oceaan B.V. January 1974 to Nigerian National Shipping Line, renamed RIVER GONGOLA. January 1980 to Candleford Shipping Co. (Cyprus) and renamed MIKELDEN.

Miami's Monarchs:
Deluxe Cruises
to the
Caribbean
and South America

23,500 tons each

VOLENDAM II & VEENDAM III (1972-1983)

Ships with chequered careers. Both were laid up due to 1974 fuel crisis. VEENDAM III chartered to Brazilian company and briefly renamed BRASIL—her sister's former name! Returned to H.A.L. as VEENDAM III. In 1975 VOLENDAM II chartered to Monarch Cruise Lines as MONARCH SUN. H.A.L. bought company in 1976 and VEENDAM III joined fleet as MONARCH STAR. By 1978 both back under H.A.L. colours and original names.

Holland America Cruises   s.s. Veendam-s.s. Volendam

VOLENDAM II & VEENDAM III (1972-1983)

Both "V"s were sold in 1983 with the advent of NIEUW AMSTERDAM III and NOORDAM III. VEENDAM III went to Bahama Cruise Lines as BERMUDA STAR whilst VOLENDAM II was sold to American Hawaii as LIBERTE. Unsuccessful, she joined her sister as CANADA STAR in 1987. Both remain in service as Commodore Cruises' ENCHANTED ISLE and ENCHANTED SEAS—few ships having borne as many different names.

Holland America's new cruise liner m.s. Prinsendam

PRINSENDAM (1973-1980)

Built by De Merwede, Hardinxveld/Giessendam. 446 one-class passengers. Completion delayed six months by shipyard fire. First ship built for Holland America Cruises and first expressly for cruises. Last Dutch-built liner for company and last to make her maiden voyage from Rotterdam (to Singapore, November 1973). Initially made year-round fortnight-long cruises to Indonesia.

PRINSENDAM (1973-1980)

From 1975 onwards, PRINSENDAM operated Alaskan cruises from Vancouver in the summer. A popular ship among those who preferred her yachtlike intimacy. Returning to Singapore at the end of her Alaskan season, she caught fire in the Gulf of Alaska, near Sitka, on 4 October 1980. 524 persons aboard safely abandoned vessel, which foundered seven days later.

NIEUW AMSTERDAM III (1983- present)

Built by Chantiers de l'Atlantique, St. Nazaire. 1,374 one-class passengers. Launched 20 August 1982, but completion plagued by problems. 26 June 1983 maiden trip postponed at last minute to 10 July, Le Havre-New York. Card posted from that voyage reads "Ship is probably best built since VISTAFJORD. Elegantly furnished. Cabin very pleasant. 417 passengers, mostly Dutch."
Sister ship: NOORDAM III

NIEUW AMSTERDAM III (1983- present)

First new H.A.L. ship in a decade. Marked the return of the famous St. Nazaire yard (builders of NORMANDIE and FRANCE) to liner construction. Combines new and traditional features, including a two-storey main lounge, walk-around open boat deck and a multi-million-dollar 17th-century Dutch art and antique collection. This card depicts the old H.A.L. logo revived with this ship and new "Ocean Liner Service" slogan which highlighted the line's traditions.

NOORDAM III (1984- present)

Built by Chantiers de l'Atlantique, St. Nazaire. 1,374 one-class passengers. Launched 21 May 1983 and maiden voyage, Le Havre-Tampa, 8 April 1984. Otherwise identical to NIEUW AMSTERDAM III, but with art and decor with a Dutch East Indies theme. The ship's characteristic flared bow with prominent knuckle is shown in this card.
Sister ship: NIEUW AMSTERDAM III

WESTERDAM II (1988- present)

Built as HOMERIC in 1985 by Jos. Meyer, Papenburg, for Home Lines. Launched 28 September 1985. 1,260 one-class passengers. Final ship for Home Lines, costing $147 mn. October 1988 to H.A.L., refitted and renamed WESTERDAM II. Built with many comparable features to the new H.A.L. vessels including a domed dining room and walk-round Boat Deck. Card posted on October 1989 voyage to Germany for "stretching" reads "More quality than expected— superior to NOORDAM on most counts. *Really* nice stateroom!"

WESTERDAM II (1988- present) (Maxwell collection)

H.A.L. decided to lengthen WESTERDAM II to increase capacity and fully upgrade her to company standards. This $65 mn. rebuilding was accomplished at the builder's yard between October 1989-March 1990 with a new 130 ft. midsection added. At 53,872 grt, she is the largest ship yet owned by the company. This card depicts the builder's model of the lengthened vessel.

SELECT BIBLIOGRAPHY

DE GROOT, Edward P., *Per Mailboot naar Amerika: Vijftig jaar Noordatlantische passagiersvaart onder Nederlandse vlag*, De Boer Maritiem, Bussum, 1980.

DE HAAS, C., *De Groote Drie: NIEUW AMSTERDAM, ORANJE en WILLEM RUYS*, de Boer Maritiem, Bussum, 1976.

HOLLAND AMERICA LIJN, *Samenspel* (house journal), Rotterdam.

KONINGS, Chris, *De NIEUW AMSTERDAM*, den Boer Uitgevers, Middelburg, 1987.

LAGENDIJK, A, *Scheepvaart van de Lage Landen: Passagiersschepen in Het Noordatlantisch Vaargebied*, Uitgevers Wyt, Rotterdam, 1976.

LE FLEMING, H. M., *Ships of the Holland-America Line*, John Marshbank, London, 1963.

MOLL, F. G. E., "History in Brief of the Nederlandsch-Amerikaansche Stoomvaart Mij–Holland America Line, Rotterdam", The Belgian Shiplover, October/November 1953.

PAYNE, Stephen M., *Grande Dame: Holland America Line and the S.S. ROTTERDAM*, Royal Institute of Naval Architects, London, 1990.

SCHAAP, Dick & Schaap, Dick, *A Bridge to the Seven Seas: the Pictorial Story of a Century of Ocean Travel Aboard Holland America Ships*, David McKay, New York, 1973.

VAN KIRK, C., *De Schepen van de Holland Amerika Lijn*, Erato, Haarlem, 1981.

INDEX

1. Roman numerals following a ship's name indicate that she is the first, second, third etc., vessel to carry that name in the fleet.

2. Dimensions are registered length × width × depth, except in cases where the overall length is quoted. For ease of reference all dimensions are rounded off to the nearest foot.

3. Gross tonnage is shown as completed or as rebuilt (see note 7). It should be noted that these figures vary by subsequent modifications or changes to the measurement rules.

4. Engine types are indicated as follows;
   Reciprocating: C = compound; T = triple expansion; Q = quadruple expansion
   Turbine: LPT = low pressure turbine; Tur = steam turbine
   Diesel: D = diesel
   A plus sign indicates combination machinery

5. Screws. The number of screws are shown thus; 1XS, 2XS etc.

6. Speed. The average speed obtained in H.A.L. service is quoted in knots.

7. Rebuilt. In the case of ships substantially modified during their careers amended details appear immediately below their first entry.

	Dimensions	Tonnage	Machinery	Speed	Page
AAGTEDYK	*455 × 62 × 28	7646	Tur 1 × S	15.6	74
AALSDYK	439 × 62 × 35	7645	Tur 1 × S	15.6	74
AARDYK	439 × 62 × 35	7643	Tur 1 × S	15.6	74
ABBEDYK	439 × 62 × 35	7640	Tur 1 × S	15.6	74
AKKRUMDYK	439 × 62 × 35	7636	Tur 1 × S	15.6	74
ALMDYK	469 × 70 × 30	8286	Tur 1 × S	16.5	74–75
AMSTELDYK	439 × 62 × 30	7648	Tur 1 × S	17	74
ANDYK II	469 × 70 × 30	8380	Tur 1 × S	16.5	71
APPINGEDYK	440 × 62 × 35	7624	Tur 1 × S	15.5	74
ARENDSDYK	439 × 62 × 30	7639	Tur 1 × S	15.6	74
ARKELDYK	439 × 62 × 30	7664	Tur 1 × S	15.6	74
ARNEDYK	439 × 62 × 30	7638	Tur 1 × S	15.6	74
AVERDYK	439 × 62 × 30	7639	Tur 1 × S	15.6	74
AXELDYLK	439 × 62 × 30	7639	Tur 1 × S	15.6	74
BEEMSTERDYK	400 × 54 × 37	6869	Tur 1 × S	12	27
BILDERDYK	400 × 54 × 37	6856	Tur 1 × S	12	27
BINNENDYK	400 × 54 × 37	6873	Tur 1 × S	12	27
BLIJDENDYK I	400 × 54 × 37	6854	Tur 1 × S	12	27
BLOMMERSDYK II	400 × 54 × 37	6855	Tur 1 × S	12	27
BOSCHDYK	400 × 54 × 37	6872	Tur 1 × S	12	27
BREEDYK	400 × 54 × 37	6861	Tur 1 × S	12	27
DALERDYK /	491 × 65 × 34	10820	D 2 × S	15	45–46
DAMSTERDYK	491 × 65 × 34	10155	D 2 × S	14.5	45–46
DELFTDYK /	*509 × 65 × 34	10220	D 2 × S	14.5	43–44
DONGEDYK	529 × 65 × 34	10942	D 2 × S	15.5	43–44
DIEMERDYK	481 × 69 × 39	11195	Tur 1 × S	17	78–79, 81, 100
DINTELDYK II	*504 × 69 × 30	10000	Tur 1 × S	16.5	78, 100
DUIVENDYK	480 × 63 × 29	8338	Tur 1 × S	14	73
EDAM IV	450 × 58 × 37	8871	Tur 1 × S	13	25
EEMDYK III	476 × 64 × 40	9894	Tur 1 × S	16	72

	Dimensions	Tonnage	Machinery	Speed	Page
GROOTE BEER	440 × 62 × 34	9140	Tur 1 × S	16	80
HOLLAND	150 × 28 × 12	446	T 1 × S	?	11
KAMPERDYK	*460 × 62 × 25	5290	D 1 × S	16	90–91
KATSEDYK	*460 × 62 × 25	5376	D 1 × S	16	90–91
KERKEDYK	*460 × 62 × 25	5324	D 1 × S	16	90–91
KINDERDYK II	*460 × 62 × 25	5634	D 1 × S	16	90–91
KLOOSTERDYK	*460 × 62 × 25	5635	D 1 × S	16	90–91
KORENDYK	*460 × 62 × 25	5290	D 1 × S	16	90–91
LEERDAM II	450 × 58 × 37	8854	Tur 1 × S	13	23–24
MAASDAM II	*432 × 41 × 34	3984	C 1 × S	13.75	1
MAASDAM III	450 × 58 × 37	8812	Tur 1 × S	13	23, 25
MAASDAM IV	482 × 69 × 38	15024	Tur 1 × S	16	81, 85–87
MAASDAM V	*719 × 101 × 25	55400	D 2 × 3	20	62
NIEUW AMSTERDAM I	600 × 69 × 36	16967	Q 2 × S	16	7–10, 57
NIEUW AMSTERDAM II	714 × 88 × 50	36287	Tur 2 × S	21	47–54, 60, 61–63
NIEUW AMSTERDAM III	*704 × 89 × 24	33930	D 2 × S	21	116–117
NOORDAM I	550 × 62 × 34	12531	T 2 × S	15	5, 56
NOORDAM II	481 × 64 × 33	10726	D 2 × S	18	64–65, 110
NOORDAM III	*704 × 89 × 24	33933	D 2 × S	21	116, 118
PENNLAND	574 × 68 × 41	16082	Q + T 3 × S	16	67
POELDYK II	413 × 54 × 21	3551	D 1 × S	16.5	111
POTSDAM	550 × 62 × 35	12522	T 2 × S	14	3
PRINSENDAM	*427 × 63 × 20	8566	D 1 × S	21	114–5
PRINSES MARGRIET	456 × 61 × 28	9336	D 1 × S	17	110
ROTTERDAM I	*270 × 35 × 29	1694	C 1 × S	10.5	55
ROTTERDAM IV	650 × 77 × 48	24200	Q 2 × S	16.5	12–19, 58
ROTTERDAM V	748 × 94 × 30	38645	Tur 2 × S	20.5	16, 19, 101–109

	Dimensions	Tonnage	Machinery	Speed	Page
RYNDAM I	550 × 62 × 26	12527	T 2 × S	15	5
RYNDAM II	482 × 69 × 39	15015	Tur 1 × S	16.5	81–85
RYNDAM III	*719 × 101 × 25	55400	D 2 × S	20	62
SCHIEDYK II	472 × 66 × 38	9592	Tur 1 × S	17	77
SEVEN SEAS	492 × 70 × 34	11733	D 1 × S	17	88–89
SLOTERDYK II	473 × 62 × 34	9230	D 2 × S	15.5	68–69
SOESTDYK II	466 × 66 × 38	9592	Tur 1 × S	17	76–77
SOMMELSDYK III	473 × 62 × 34	9227	D 2 × S	15.5	68
SPAARNDAM I	*443 × 42 × 33	4539	C 1 × S	13	1
SPAARNDAM II	450 × 58 × 37	8857	Tur 1 × S	13	26
STATENDAM I	529 × 60 × 42	10491	T 2 × S	14.5	2
STATENDAM II	*764 × 86 × 58	32234	Q + T 3 × S	17	20–22
STATENDAM III	674 × 81 × 49	28291	Tur 2 × S	19	35–42
STATENDAM IV	*642 × 79 × 26	24300	Tur 2 × S	19	92, 99, 104
STATENDAM V	*719 × 101 × 25	55451	D 2 × S	20	62
VEENDAM I	*430 × 41 × 34	3707	C 1 × S	13.5	1
VEENDAM II	550 × 67 × 41	15450	T 2 × S	15	31–34, 59
VEENDAM III	*617 × 84 × 54	23372	T 2 × S	20.5	61, 112–113
VOLENDAM I	550 × 67 × 41	15434	T 2 × S	15	28–30
VOLENDAM II	*617 × 84 × 54	23395	T 2 × S	20.5	61, 112–113
WESTERDAM I	496 × 66 × 37	12149	D 2 × S	17.5	70
WESTERDAM II	*669 × 95 × 24	42092	D 2 × S	22.5	119–120
	*798 × 95 × 24	53872	D 2 × S	22.5	119–120
WESTERNLAND	574 × 68 × 41	16479	Q + T 3 × S	16	66 – 67
ZAANDAM II	481 × 64 × 36	10909	D 2 × S	18	64–65
ZUIDERDAM	496 × 66 × 37	12150	D 2 × S	17.5	70

(never completed)

Two cards from The Sterling collection, a 1930s poster featuring STATENDAM and a 1914 advertising card featuring ROTTERDAM IV making the first ever cruise by a Holland America ship.